FAIRY TALES

ALSO BY ROBERT WALSER
FROM NEW DIRECTIONS

Robert Walser

FAIRY TALES
DRAMOLETTES

With a foreword by Reto Sorg

*Translated from the German
by Daniele Pantano
and James Reidel*

A NEW DIRECTIONS PAPERBOOK

Design by Erik Rieselbach
Manufactured in the United States of America
New Directions Books are printed on acid-free paper.
First published as a New Directions Paperbook (NDP1313) in 2015

Library of Congress Cataloging-in-Publication Data
Walser, Robert, 1878–1956, author.
[Plays. Selections. English]
Fairytales : dramolettes / Robert Walser with a foreword by Reto Sorg ;
translated by Daniele Pantano and James Reidel.
pages cm.
ISBN 978-0-8112-2398-0 (acid-free paper)
I. Pantano, Daniele, translator. II. Reidel, James, translator. III. Title.
PT2647.A64A2 2015
832'.912—dc23   2014036422

10 9 8 7 6 5 4 3 2 1

New Directions Books are published for James Laughlin
by New Directions Publishing Corporation
80 Eighth Avenue, New York 10011

CONTENTS

FOREWORD

"Cinderella, she seems so easy."
Bob Dylan, "Desolation Row"

In his hometown of Biel, where he was born in 1878 and which he left in 1895, Robert Walser discovered his passion for the theater. Inspired by Friedrich Schiller, he dreamed of becoming an actor and playwright. As a writer, Walser retained and masterfully cultivated this histrionic passion for the spoken word. He expressed, imitated, and perfectly adapted the immediate presence of speech into writing, which also complemented his arsenal for irony.

Walser is not an author who strives in the free and open. "We are so glad in dark, meditative holes," he wrote in 1907 in his essay "The Theater, a Dream." He loved the delimited and well-defined space. Restriction allowed him to compress and unfold his imaginarium. Since his youth, Walser knew that the magical effect of literature finds its most wonderful expression in the theater. "Are the fictions not dreams, and isn't the open stage nothing other than its wide-open mouth talking in its sleep?"

Although Walser admired the theater, he never wrote directly for the stage. Instead, he imparted a theatrical *Grundgestus* in his prose (Brecht's word meaning fundamental gesture, attitude, posture), which the fairy-tale dramolettes—translated here by Daniele Pantano and James Reidel—also demonstrate. They are short, closet plays that do not retell the familiar fairy tale but rather recall their symbols and tropes. "Whether they could ever be put on with, for instance, music is totally questionable and seems for the present utterly beside the point. They are tempered for speech and language, to a beat and a rhythmic enjoyment," Walser wrote to a publisher in 1912.

As it turned out, Walser's fairy-tale dramolettes found their way to the stage during the 1970s, when young troupes and little theaters discovered them. Representing a milestone in the history of their reception is Heinz Holliger's opera *Snow White (Schneewittchen)*, which is based on Walser's text and premiered at the Zurich Opera House in 1998 with great success. Originally, in 1901, *Cinderella (Aschenbrödel)* and *Snow White* were published in the journal *Die Insel*. In 1919, Walser gathered them with other dramolettes for the volume *Comedies*. Around the same time he likely wrote *Thorn Rose (Dornröschen)*, or *Sleeping Beauty*, which appeared a year later in the journal *Pro Helvetia. The Christ Child (Das Christkind)*, also dates from that time and was published in *Die Neue Rundschau* in 1920. It can be read too as a fairy tale or, more properly, a verse morality.

During Walser's lifetime these publications received very little real public reaction. An exception is Walter Benjamin who, in his 1929 essay on Walser, called *Snow White* "one of the most profound creations of recent literature and one that is sufficient on its own to show why the most playful of all writers was a favorite of the merciless Franz Kafka." Benjamin continues, "Walser starts where the fairy tales stop. 'And if they are not dead, they live now.' Walser shows *how* they live."

Looking at literary history, Walser's fairy-tale dramolettes are not unique. They belong to adaptations, re-creations, collections, and studies in the field of folk and literary fairy tales that have been treated by different minds such as Carlo Collodi, Oscar Wilde, L. Frank Baum, Engelbert Humperdinck, Johann Strauss, Selma Lagerlöf, Blaise Cendrars, Carl Einstein, Franz Kafka, Hugo von Hofmannsthal, and Carl Jung.

The fairy-tale dramolettes are magical literary theater—"entirely poetry" in Walser's words. The characters, while still fairy-tale beings, exemplify the modern individual who exists to understand the possible terms of his or her fate. For the characters, the fairy tale is the world and language out of which they are made, their nature. Walser depicts self-knowledge as an existential state of poetic exaggeration. When the characters speak of their existence, they stand as if beside themselves. Everything has already happened; time has stopped; life becomes reflectively stretched apart. It is transformed into this dream reality, which is fantastic, disillusioning, demonic, enchanting, enlightening, and uplifting. In addition to the subject matter and the metatheatrical dimension is Walser's inimitable language that gives the dramolettes their special charm. For all its simplicity and elegance, his language is dazzling and full of surprising, ironic twists:

> The language must be a weasel
> falling headlong when it wishes
> that it didn't lack words for her,
> but it can see her poverty.

These days we have learned to deal with the ambivalence of the tableau. Together with innovation, making the unreal means a threatening alienation as well. Walser, however, belongs to a generation that welcomes illusion. Fiction appears as a romantic power that allows one to transform a mundane reality:

> Isn't reality a dream too?
> Aren't we all, even when awake,
> going about a bit like dreamers,
> sleepwalkers in the light of day,
> who play around with caprices
> and act as if awake?

While they are jubilantly playful, the fairy-tale dramolettes are little teaching plays too. The characters behave as if in a poetic purgatory, twisting and turning until they confess, which in the end is precisely their purpose. They are messengers of a poetic existence who bear witness to the human longing for being without boundaries while rooted in a center. As an enlightened poet, Walser knew where the power of poetry exists. This is revealed by the Fairy Tale, as a character herself:

> The people don't believe in me,
> but so what when just my nearness
> makes them think a little again.

RETO SORG

ROBERT WALSER-ZENTRUM, BERN

TRANSLATORS' NOTE

The source text for these translations is Robert Walser, *Komödie: Märchenspiele und szenische Dichtungen* (1986). Occasional notes are provided to enhance reading and understanding. The order of the first three plays is not chronological, but rather that of a dramatic or cinematic trilogy-triptych, one that allows the reader to challenge, in a small, Walserian way, the culturally hegemonic Disney cartoon adaptations of the past midcentury (and reinforced once more with the 2014 film *Maleficent*).

As to the titles, *Snow White* is a virtual cognate of the German title. *Cinderella*, however, is from the familiar French version of the tale by Charles Perrault—*Cendrillon*—which means the same as the German word *Aschenbrödel*, a scullion maid. (The second part of the word/name is from the verb *brodeln*, or *prudeln*, literally to seethe, boil, sputter, and figuratively to talk too much, which Walser exploits here.) *Thorn Rose*—which alludes to the heroine's "thorny" quality—would be lost in the title that has supplanted it over time. Thus, "Sleeping Beauty" appears in the translation's subtitle.

The inclusion here of *The Christ Child* is our inescapable assertion that Walser intended it as a fairy tale, too, given all the devotion to the original text as the other three.

J.R. & D.P.

SNOW WHITE

A garden. To the right the palace entrance.
In the background rolling mountains.
The Queen, Snow White, the foreign Prince, the Hunter.

Queen:

Say, are you sick?

Snow White:

You would ask since you wanted death
on the one who ever stung you
in the eyes as too beautiful.
How you look at me so composed.
This kindness, showing in your eyes,
so full of love, is just made up,
the serene tone just counterfeit.
Hate really does dwell in your heart.
You dispatched the Hunter to me
and told him to draw his dagger,
to point it at this despised face.
You ask me whether I'm sick now?
Such sport sounds bad from a soft voice.
Indeed, softness becomes sly sport
when it is so fearlessly cruel.
I'm not sick; I'm very much dead.
The poison apple was painful,
O, O so painful, and Mother, you,
you're the one who brought it to me.
So why joke about my being sick?

Queen:

Fair child, you are wrong. You are sick,
no, gravely, very gravely ill.

There's no doubt this fresh garden air
will do you good. I beg of you,
just don't let your weak little head
give in to the idea. Be still.
Don't mull things over and over.
Get some exercise, skip and run.
Shout racing for a butterfly.
Scold the air for not making it
warm enough yet. Become a child.
Soon you'll leave this color behind,
which is like a pale winding sheet
draped over your pink complexion.
Think not of sin. The sin should be
forgotten. Perhaps I did sin
against you many long years ago.
Who could remember such a thing?
Unpleasant things are easily
forgotten if you consider
who's near and dear. Are you crying?

Snow White:
Yes, I must when I realize
how quick you are to wring the past
by the neck the way you wanted
mine wrung. Crying, of course, over
the sinful absent mind that wants
to sweet-talk me. O how you give
this sin such wings, and yet it flies
terribly with this new pair
that do not fit. It lies so close
to me and you, this thing you want
bantered away with a sweet word,
so close, I'd say, close to the touch,
such that I can never forget it,
nor you who committed it.
Hunter, speak, you did swear my death?

Hunter:

> Of course, princess, a grisly death,
> just not performed as loud and clear
> as the fairy tale made public.
> The humble way you begged touched me,
> your face, lying there sweet as snow
> beneath the kiss of the sunlight.
> I sheathed that which I intended
> for your murder, stabbing the deer
> that leapt across our path. I sucked
> the blood out of him greedily.
> Yours, however, I left untouched.
> So don't say I swore you should die.
> I took pity and broke my oath
> before I did you any harm.

Queen:

> So what are you crying about?
> He drew his dagger as a joke.
> He'd have to stab what's soft in him
> before he could ever stab you.
> But he didn't. The soft in him
> is alive like the morning sun.
> Come give me a kiss and forget.
> Look up with joy and show some sense.

Snow White:

> How can I kiss the lips of one
> who pushed this Hunter off, kissed him
> into doing the bloody deed.
> I'll never kiss you. With kisses
> you fired the Hunter to murder
> and my death was seconds away,
> because he was your sweet lover.

Queen:

> What did you say?

Hunter:

>Me with kisses?

Prince:

>I really believe it's all true.
>That man in the green jacket has
>far less respect than befits him
>in the presence of this great Queen.
>Snow White, O how evilly have
>you been played by such ruthless hate.
>It's a wonder that you're alive.
>You survived poison and a knife.
>From what stuff are you made,
>for you're dead and yet so lovely
>alive, indeed, so little dead
>that life must be in love with you?
>Tell me, did this Hunter stab you?

Snow White:

>No, no, there beats in this fellow
>a good heart filled with compassion.
>If the Queen had this heart, she would
>be a better mother to me.

Queen:

>I mean to be much better with you
>than your keen suspicion suggests.
>I did not send the Hunter off
>after you with kisses. Blind fear
>has made you too apprehensive.
>In fact, I have always loved you
>as my sweet, innocent child.
>Why would I have any reason,
>cause, or right to hate one as dear
>to me as a child of my own breast!
>O do not believe that coy voice

that whispers of sin, which it's not.
Believe your right, not your left ear,
I mean that false one telling you
that I am this evil mother
green-eyed at beauty. Don't be fooled
by such an absurd fairy tale
stuffing the world's greedy ears full
of these newsy bits that I am
mad with jealousy, by nature
evil. It is just idle talk.
I love you. To admit this has
never been said more sincerely.
That you're so lovely gives me joy.
Beauty in one's own child is balm
for a mother's love gone weary,
not the goad to some heinous deed,
like the fairy tale has laid out
for this story line here, this play.
Don't turn away. Be a dear child.
Trust a parent's word as your own.

Snow White:

O I believed you with pleasure,
for believing is quiet bliss.
But how much faith is going to make
me believe when no faith exists,
where a roguish malice lurks, where
injustice sits with a proud neck?
You speak as kindly as you can,
and yet you still cannot act kind.
Those eyes, flashing so scornfully,
wince at me so threatening, so
unmotherly, laugh with menace
at the affection on your tongue,
with derision. They speak the truth,

and they alone, those proud eyes, I
believe, not the backstabber's tongue.

Prince:

I believe you see right, my child.

Queen:

Must you keep helping, little prince,*
feeding more flames to the fire, where
a flood of healing is needed?
A stranger clad in motley clothes
should not step too close to a queen.

Prince:

Why not dare to rise against you,
you fiend, for the princess's sake?

Queen:

What?

Prince:

Yes, and while I look small and weak,
I'll echo this a thousand times,
ten—a hundred thousand times for you:
a dreadful crime's taken place here,
and one that points to you, the Queen.
Poison was strewn for this sweet child,
set out as though she were a dog.
Why not admit your wickedness,
your good conscience! You, fair child,
let's go up for a little while
and contemplate this grievous thing.
If you're too weak, just lay your head

* The Prince should be seen as shorter than the other characters,
even Snow White, and wearing a checkered costume.

upon my faithful shoulder here,
which would cherish such a burden.
From you, Queen, we shall take our leave
for now of a short span of time.
Then we'll continue our talk.
                    (To Snow White) Come,
permit me this sweet liberty.

> *He leads her inside the palace.*

Queen:

Just go, broken mast and rigging.
Go newlyweds, married to death.
Go misery, lead weakness away,
and be very dear arm in arm.
Come, fair Hunter, let's have a talk.

> *Change of scene. A room inside the palace. The Prince*
> *and Snow White.*

Prince:

I would talk away the whole day
with you and do so arm in arm.
How strange this language is to me
that comes from that sweet mouth of yours.
Your mere word, how alive it is.
My ear hangs rapt on its richness
in a hammock of harkening,
while dreaming of a violin strain,
a lisp, a fair nightingale's song,
of love's twittering. In and out
the dreaming goes like ocean waves
washing onto our garden shore.
O speak, and I'm ever asleep,
a prisoner of love this way,

in chains, yet infinitely rich,
free as no free man ever was.

Snow White:

You speak such noble princely speech.

Prince:

No, let me listen instead,
so that the love I swore below
in the garden, in that playpen,
never blows away in vain words.
I only want to listen and respond
to your love that sounds in my head.
Speak, that I am ever silent
and true to you. Unfaithfulness
comes quick with words. It speaks rashly,
a fountain in the wind, being whipped,
to froth over into babble.
No, let me be silent, true to you.
In this sense I shall love you more
than with love. Then wholeheartedness
knows itself no more. It showers
me in wetness the same as you.
Love is wet the way the night is,
such that dry dust never clouds it.
So speak, such that when you speak
it falls like dew upon our love.
You're quiet. What do you see there?

Snow White:

You do talk like a waterfall
of silence, yet you're not silent.

Prince:

What's wrong, speak! You look so somber,
so plaintive right down to your toes,

as if you were searching for words
that whisper love. Do not sulk there.
Speak up when something troubles you.
Unroll it just like a carpet
on which we will merrily play.
To dally in heartache does one good.

Snow White:
You talk forever and promise
silence though. What are you saying,
talking headlong on and on?
Confidence is not so quick-tongued.
Love fancies it soft and serene.
O if you're not devoted
to my bliss in every sense,
then say so. Say it, for you say
unfaithfulness would talk away
eagerly, talkative, so fast.

Prince:
Let us drop that.

Snow White:
Yes, let's make small talk, be merry.
Let us banish from love's kingdom
melancholy and dolefulness.
Let's jest and dance and cheer aloud.
Why worry of the pain of now,
which commands us to be silent!
Well, what see you in the garden?

Prince (looking out the window):
Alas, what I see is fair and sweet
to the naked eye that but sees.
To feeling, which takes in this scene
with its fine net, it is sacred.

To intellect, which knows the past,
it's disgusting, a dirty flood
of muddy water. Oh, it takes
a twofold view, sweet and terrible,
thoughtful and beautiful. Look there,
with your own eyes, see for yourself.

Snow White:

No, say, what's going on? Just tell me.
From your lips then I could gather
such a picture's subtle detail.
If you paint it, surely you will
cleverly, prudently temper
the view's poignancy. Now, what goes?
Rather than look, I'd rather hear.

Prince:

It is the most lovely passion
that ever inflamed two lovers.
The Queen kisses the Hunter's lips,
and he gives kiss after kiss back.
They sit beneath the willow tree,
whose long branches flutter downward
on both their heads. The grass kisses
the tangle of interlocked feet.
The wood bench sighs under the press
of their bodies making one body
in the rapture of their embrace.
O, so a tiger pair would mate
in the jungle, far from the real world.
The sweet bliss makes them one, tears them
apart just to bring them closer
all over again. I'm speechless,
imageless at such an image.
Will you see it and be speechless?

Snow White:

>No, such a thing would disgust me.
>Come away from that filthy scene.

Prince:

>The colors barely release me
>from its spell. It is a painting,
>and sweet love is its painter.
>O, how she lies down there, this Queen,
>being crushed inside his strong arms.
>How she cries from passion and how
>her beau smothers her with kisses,
>like one smothering a bowl of food,
>no, a sky, this mouth opening
>on heavenly passion itself.
>That rogue is utterly shameless.
>He thinks his green hunting jacket
>protects him from barbs. Here's a barb,
>what seems to bewitch me up here.
>O, I'm furious. It's this woman!
>Not this wretch. O, just that woman!
>Something does wrong to that crude wretch.
>Alas, this sweet, this sweet woman.—
>If I could only lose the sense
>of what I saw. Now I'm lost.
>A storm rages above it all,
>what is called love, wishes being called,
>but no longer. Go, everything.

Snow White:

>Woe unto me that I must hear.

Prince:

>Woe unto us that I must see.

Snow White:

> O, how I long for nothing more
> than to be smiling and dead, dead.
> This I am too and always was.—
> I've never felt life's seething storm.
> I feel as still as this soft snow
> that lies for a ray of sunlight
> that accepts it. I'm snow this way—
> and melt away with a warm breeze
> meant not for me but for the spring.
> Sweet is this seeping down. Dear earth,
> receive me unto your dwelling!
> The sun is too painful for me.

Prince:

> Do I give you this terrible pain?

Snow White:

> O no, not you. You could never!

Prince:

> How lovely you are, how you laugh
> for me, come smiling! Don't love me.
> I simply disturb your repose.
> O, to have left your coffin alone!
> How beautiful you lay therein,
> snow in a silent winter world.

Snow White:

> Snow, always snow?

Prince:

> Forgive me, you dear winter scene,
> you likeness of serene white calm.
> If I upset you, it happened
> only for love. Now this love turns
> away from you again weeping,

toward the Queen. Please forgive this love
for lifting you from that coffin,
the glass one, wherein you lay
with rosy cheeks, an open mouth,
and this breath just like one alive,
this picture to die for most sweet.
I should have left it just like that,
with love kneeling before you then.

Snow White:

Look, look! Now that I am alive
you dump me like a dead body!
How very strange you men all are.

Prince:

Rightly scold me. You're being tender.
Hate me and I'll kneel before you.
If you called me a rotten knave
it would fit well. But let me now
find that lovely Queen, for I wish
to free her from a love unworthy.
I beg of you, be very cross
with me, indeed, be very mad.

Snow White:

Why then? Give me a reason why?

Prince:

Well, because I'm such a villain
to run from you to another,
she who excites his mind more now.

Snow White:

You are not a villain! Well, well—
that mind, that mind of yours is more
excited? What's on your mind is so
mindless. What a pack of dogs must

excite your mind such that you flee
like a terrified deer, the foe
pursuing you. Well, so be it.
So fly from me then to this stream
with the better water to lap.
I'll remain, smiling, teasing you
with my pale white hand outstretched,
follow your flight with a gay voice
that calls: Snow White shall wait for you.
Come, knock on this familiar door
and laugh aloud. And then you turn
your dear, faithful head to me
begging me to just be quiet,
for shouting serves no purpose.—Go!
O go then, for I release you.
And do commend me to my Queen.

Prince:

Commend you to the Queen? What for?
Am I dreaming?

Snow White:

Well, am I not allowed to send
my regards to Mommy with you,
who's down there in that shady park
occupied with her needlework?
She sews a token of her love—
what do I care. I owe her love,
and love sends its regards with you.
Say, I forgive her. No, not that.
Anyway, it doesn't show well
for a child to be on her knees
and begging for me to forgive.
You'll be half love's own already
on your knees. Then say it like so,

in passing, like sugared pastry,
and pay heed when she nods so fair,
when she's choking with emotion
and gives her hand for your hot kiss,
which sends, you being so chivalrous,
my forgiveness for this mistake.
How impatient I am for word
from my mother. So be quick, go!

Prince:

Snow White, I don't understand you.

Snow White:

That has nothing to do with it.
Go now, I beg of you. Leave this
flower to herself that can only
bloom in full in her solitude.
For she was never meant for you;
so calm down then. Depart, leave me
to dream here, to close myself up
as though some gaily colored plant.
Go to this other flower, go,
draw upon her sweeter fragrance.

Prince:

You should calm down. Just wait here.
I shall bring the Queen back to you
reconciled. I'll look for her now
down there in her shady garden
and talk to that villain Hunter.
No matter where and when and how,
I'll find him too. So until then,
just remain calm and wait for us.

Exits.

Snow White:

> He's filled with turmoil and counsels
> calm in me that in richer measure
> than his has possession of me.
> Everything goes the way it must.
> This untrue prince has done me wrong.
> But I'll not cry, the same way
> I would not rejoice had I proof
> of his innermost love for me.
> Fury more than fury musters
> I cannot do, and who silently
> keeps silent chokes down fear, so
> this I will do. Oh my, here comes
> Mother herself and all alone.

> *To the Queen, who enters.*

> O kind mother, O forgive me.

> *She throws herself at her feet.*

Queen:

> What is this for, my child? Get up.

Snow White:

> No, on my knees like this for you.

Queen:

> What's with you, what makes you this way,
> what is trembling so in your breast?
> Stand up and tell me what is wrong.

Snow White:

> Do not withdraw this gentle hand
> that I would cover with kisses.
> How much have I longed for its squeeze!
> A shyer plea for forgiveness
> has never been made as shyly
> as mine to you. Forget, forgive.

Please be my merciful mother.
Let me be your good little girl
who clasps frightened to your body.
O sweet hand, I had thought of you,
you coming for my life, offering
me the apple: something not true.
Sin so fine is only contrived
of recalling all kinds of things.
My thinking is the only sin
there is here. O please absolve me
of the suspicion that wronged you.
I only want to love, love you.

Queen:

What? Did I not send the Hunter?
Did I not spur him on with kisses
to you to do this great, great sin?
You know that you're not thinking right.

Snow White:

I just feel! A feeling thinks sharp.
It knows every little detail
of this matter. A feeling,
far more noble than to recall,
will think a situation through,
but to forgive. And its judgment,
which is devoid of all judgment,
judges more severe, simply too.
So I see nothing in thinking.
It just speculates here and there,
full of big airs and opinions,
says this happened like so and keeps
making petty condemnations.
Away with the judge who but thinks!
If he can't feel, he must think small.

His verdict makes a belly ache.
It's bland and drives the plaintiff mad.
It absolves the sinner of sin,
dropping the charges in one breath.
Go and fetch me this other judge,
that sweet, ignorant feeling. Hear
what it says. Oh, it says nothing.
It smiles, it kisses the sin dead,
caresses it like its sister,
chokes it with kisses. My feeling
absolves you of all sin. It lies
before you on beseeching knees
and begs, calls me sinner, me who
pleads so frightened for forgiveness.

Queen:

The poison apple I sent you;
you took a bite, of course, and died.
The dwarfs bore you in the coffin,
the one of glass, until the kiss
of the Prince brought you back to life.
That is what happened, am I right?

Snow White:

All of it's true up to the kiss.
The defiling mouth of a man
has never before kissed these lips.
The Prince, and how he could kiss too—
he had no hair upon his chin.
He's still a little boy, elsewise
noble, but so very short, weak,
like the body he's trapped inside,
small, like the mind he depends on.
Of one prince's kiss say nothing more
of it, Mommy. The kiss is dead,

for he never sensed the wetness
on both sides of two moistened lips.
What did I want to talk about?
Ah, of sin, that stands on its knees,
before you, of the dear sinner.

Queen:
No, that is wrong. You yourself tell
fairy-tale lies. Surely it
says that I am an evil queen,
that I dispatched the Hunter to you,
and gave you the apple to eat.
Now answer me straight about this.
Your begging me for forgiveness
is just a joke, isn't that right?
All of this gesture and technique
is rehearsed, a script cleverly
practiced by you yourself. You have,
as it turns out, only made me
suspicious. What are you doing now?

Snow White:
Looking upon your kind, soft hand,
seeing its beauty wondrously
waking in a child a feeling
almost totally extinguished.
No, you are no sinner at all:
where would you get this idea?
Neither am I. We're still spotless
of all guilt, immaculately
watching an immaculate sky
being as mild as it has been here.
Once we did evil to ourselves.
But that is far too long ago
to remember. Now part for me,

I beg you, those dear lips of yours.
Tell me something very happy.

Queen:

I sent you off to die sparing
not one kiss or caress on him,
who followed you like a wild beast,
hunting you through woods and fields
until you fell down to the ground.

Snow White:

Ah, yes, I know the story well,
about the apple, the coffin.
Be so kind as to tell me more.
Why does nothing else come to mind?
Must you hang on to these details?
Must you forever draw on them?

Queen:

With kisses, kisses I fired on
the Hunter, my bloodthirsty man.
O, how the kisses came raining
like drops of dew upon that face
swearing faith to me, harm to you.

Snow White:

Forget about it, my dear Queen.
I beg you think no more of it.
Do not roll your big eyes like that.
Why do you shake? You've only
been good to me all of your life,
for which I'm utterly grateful.
If love knew of a better word,
then it might speak less awkwardly.
Love is boundless for that reason.
It knows to say nothing when it's

wholly enrapt in your being.
Hate me so that I can but love
more childlike, more wholeheartedly
and lovingly by myself,
for no other reason than that
love is sweet and ambrosial
to one who humbly offers it.
Don't you hate me?

Queen:

I hate myself much more than you.
Once I did hate you, begrudging
your beauty despite the whole world,
for the whole world sang your praises,
gave you homage while I, the Queen,
was looked upon suspiciously.
O did that make my blood boil.
It turned me into this tigress.
I didn't see with my own eyes.
I didn't hear with my own ears.
Unfounded hate but saw and heard,
ate, dreamt, performed, and slept for me.
I lay sadly upon my ear,
doing what it did. That's in the past.
Hate now wants to love. And love hates
itself for not loving harder.
Why look, there comes the young Prince.
Go, kiss him, call him your precious.
Tell him I shall be nice to him
despite his bitter words spoken
in your favor. Go and tell him!

The Prince enters.

Prince:

Fair Queen, I've been looking for you.

Queen:

>Fair? This is a polite greeting.
>I do like you, Prince, Snow White's half,
>to whom you wish to be married.

Prince:

>Snow White wants not to be my bride.
>She says I've had a change of mind
>since lifting her from the coffin
>and leading her here. She is right
>to blame it all on you, Queen. To you
>I utterly devote myself.

Queen:

>Where is this weak temperament,
>which like a reed shakes back and forth
>when the wind blows, going to take us?

Prince:

>Where? I don't really know where.
>But this I know only too well,
>that I am in love, and with whom?
>With you, with the Queen that you are.

Queen:

>Such love, ah, that doesn't suit me.
>This is too fast. Your behavior
>I find perfectly juvenile.
>Your mind is far too capricious,
>your nature too rash. Have patience
>and don't tell me that you love me.
>In fact, you need to be scolding me
>still, Snow White's half, she whom you seem
>to rather carelessly forget.
>Hey, Hunter.

Prince:

>What of that villain?

Queen:

He's no villain. In hunter's clothes,
he equals ten thousand princes.
Don't be a hothead. Think of who's
present when you stir up your storm.

To the Hunter, who appears.

Oh, there you are.

Hunter:

What's your bidding?

Queen:

As though it were real, reenact
that scene of Snow White's distress
that she had in the forest here.
Do so as though you wished to kill.
You, girl, beg as though you mean it.
Me and the Prince, we will just watch
and critique if you play your roles
too lightly. Now then, let's begin!

Hunter:

Snow White, come, I'm going to kill you.

Snow White:

Oh, like it happened that quickly.
First draw your dagger. I'm not scared
at all of your proud booming voice.
Why do you want to strangle me,
this life you see here, who never
caused you injury or insult?

Hunter:

The Queen hates you. She bid me here
to kill. Ferociously she drove
me to it with her sweet kisses.

Queen:

Ha, ha, with kisses, ha, ha, ha.

Snow White:

>Is anything amiss, dear Queen?

Queen:

>Nothing, play on. You're doing just fine.

Prince:

>The villain does the villain's role
>like second nature. It fits him
>as tight as his hunter's costume.

Queen:

>Prince, Prince!

Hunter (to Snow White):

>Now then, prepare yourself to die.
>Don't give me any trouble, please.
>You're just sand in the Queen's eyes.
>You must leave this beautiful world.
>This she wills, this she bid me do.
>Be done! Why are you drawing back?

Snow White:

>Can't I fight off this brazen death
>when it's grabbing me by my throat?
>Are you death, O hard-hearted man!
>I don't believe it. You look kind.
>A sweet nature dwells on your brows.
>You kill animals, not people
>who're not your open enemy.
>I do see this. Mercy makes you
>put the knife back. Thank you, thank you!
>Would but the Queen have your nature.

Queen:

>So? Really? You're dead serious.
>Do you forget and speak the truth?—

Then, Hunter, please step from this role.
It's unbefitting such a man.
Run the evil whore through, right now.
For the entire afternoon
she's been hectoring me with her
two-faced blathering. O slay her.
Bring that lying heart of hers here
and lay it down at your Queen's feet.

The Hunter points his dagger at Snow White.

Prince:

What, what is going on? Snow White, run.
Stop that you, you villain. O Queen,
what a snake you are after all.

Queen (laughing at the Hunter while stopping his arm):

All of this is only a game.
Come into the garden. Spring air,
rising, falling in the park's shade,
chatting along the graveled path,
is the bickering's happy end.
I must be a snake in your eyes,
nothing but evil. No matter,
for the next hour will prove to you
that I am not. Snow White, come.
Prince, if you will allow me now,
I shall call her my dear child.
We were just pretending before!
Trust me, and you played your parts well.
That was just for fun, a dagger
waved around in a hunter's hand.
So he's the villain—ha, ha, ha.
Come, come all into the garden.

Prince:

But I still don't quite trust you yet.

Queen:

Come, little rabbit prince! Come too,
Hunter. Laughter will lead the way.

Hunter:

Indeed, my Queen.

They exit.

Change of scene. A garden like the one in the first scene. The Queen and Snow White enter.

Queen:

You lament again as before,
are bitter, and give me this sad look.
Why such a change without a word?
You know I don't hold any grudge.
You have no reason to be sad.
Once more the Prince has turned to you
in love anew and yet you sulk
and don't see that love's drawing near,
approaching you from every side.

Snow White:

Oh, but the thought of you hating
and pursuing me I can't shed.
In my troubled mind it follows
me and never, so long as I live,
can I get this out of my mind.
It sticks like this black in my heart.
It darkens every joyful note
of my soul and I am so tired.
I long for that open coffin,

laid out as this frozen image.
Were I but with my dwarfs, then
I would have peace and give you yours.
I plague you. I see you want me
a thousand miles away from here.

Queen:
No, no.

Snow White:
Ah, if I could be with the dwarfs.

Queen:
How was it there? Nice and quiet?

Snow White:
There sleep lays as quiet as snow.
I would be with them, like brothers
they were and so kind; there it shines,
having a cheerful cleanliness.
Pain, like some foul leftover food,
unpleasant to a refined sense,
was strange to that life's white table.
Like a bedsheet, the happiness
was so clean you fell into sleep,
into this realm of colored dreams.
Unknown among the people there
was any ungenerous nature.
Each cherished their gentility,
good manners. Sweet conversations
found upon their lips a response.
I would still be there, but I was
driven in tears to you again,
back into this world where a heart
has to wither away and die.

Queen:

>So among your dwarfs hate did not
>exist? Perhaps love to them, too,
>was something entirely foreign.
>As you know, hate nourishes love,
>and love rather prefers to love,
>as you well know, cold, bitter hate.

Snow White:

>I never felt a harsh word there.
>Hate never tarnished love. If love
>was there, that I don't really know.
>Hate makes love perceptible first.
>There I didn't know what love was.
>Here I know, for there's just hate here.
>My yearning for love had made me
>conscious of love; inspired by hate,
>a soul longs to find love in some place.
>And there it dwelled among the dwarfs
>in unadulterated joy.
>No more about it. That was then.

Queen:

>Now then, my dear, let's have a laugh.

Snow White:

>No, laughing wants some delight
>other than what is in my breast.
>My delight is only to cry.
>With kisses and flattery
>you goaded the Hunter just now,
>spurred him on to murder. You said,
>"Run the evil whore through," shaking
>with anger. You called it a game.
>O, how the desire for revenge
>drove that outrageous game with me,

she who knows not how to fight back.
Lower me into my grave. Then
Snow White's grave is Snow White's delight.
I only find delight smiling
in my coffin. There is my joy.
Please lay me beside it.

Queen:

Now you smile, indeed, you're laughing.

Snow White:

Ah, if only for a moment.
This other thing tells me once more
about the pain and woe you cause.
It wags with its finger, points long,
and shows me with enormous eyes
what you're up to. Then it whispers,
"Your mother is not your mother."
The world is never a sweet world.
Love is a leery, wordless hate.
A hunter's a prince. Life is death.
You are not a good queen, rather
you are a proud and wanton one
who dispatched my bloody Hunter.
He's dear to you. You flattered him.
You granted him that one sweet kiss
with which you drove him to the kill.
I am his quarry—all of this
speaks of the next bitter moment.
Now you shall hate me twice over.

Queen:

I set him on fire with kisses.
Didn't I? Isn't that so? Say it!
Shout it loud in this gentle world,
into the winds and echo it

into the clouds. Carve it likewise
into these tree trunks rank with leaves,
breathe it into these gentle airs
that they, with this subtle fragrance,
broadcast it likewise into spring.
O, then everyone sucks it up,
praising you as the innocent,
calling me the terrible one
for I fed this murder with love,
inflamed it with a poison kiss.
Hey there, Hunter, where'd you go? Come.
Leave this guilt behind. I'll kiss you,
call you the dearest man of all,
the best, the truest, the strongest and
the handsomest, the boldest man.
Snow White, help me here in my praise.

Snow White:

Enough, enough, you are going mad.
Had I only not opened up
the poisoned wound. Now it's bleeding
fresh again and will never heal.
If you would but forgive me, Queen.

Queen:

To hell with forgiveness, guilt, shame,
going soft. Hey, my loyal servant!

The Hunter appears.

Hunter:

Did you call, Your Highness?

Queen:

My one and only, let's kiss first.
I could die. However, I still
should have this short conversation.

I still need to explain this game,
otherwise she, who it concerns,
will call it crude. Talk in my place.
Explain to this silly, sad-eyed girl here
that I hate and love her as well.
Show your dagger. No don't, darling!
Just let it remain in its sheath.
You should only talk, comfort her,
tell her something she can believe,
and reassure me, make it all
quiet again as it had been
before this casual game began.
Now let's get on with it, and do
watch yourself. Don't say too little
that your spare words don't say too much.

Hunter:
    Snow White, come over here to me.

Snow White:
    Since I'm no longer scared, gladly.

Hunter:
    Do you think I want to kill you?

Snow White:
    Yes and yet no. Yes, I'm strangled.
    No swiftly tells me yes again.
    Say it so that I believe you,
    that I must believe forever.
    No makes me tired. Yes is lovely.
    I believe the things you say, too.
    I like to say: Yes, I believe.
    No has long been averse to me.
    Thus, yes, yes, I do believe you.

Hunter:

Now see, that's the voice of Snow White.
She's not herself being suspicious,
torturess torturing herself
and those who are devotedly
in love with her. Let me say now,
this suspicion just tells a lie,
a made-up, poisonous lie, so,
Snow White, believe me. It's not true!

Snow White:

Yes, how gladly so. O yes, why
not yes to all that you say.
Saying yes feels so good, is so
endlessly sweet. I believe you.
Yes, if you were to lie, to build
the fairy tale into the sky,
tell me lies, draw me a picture
within reach crudely, awkwardly,
I would believe you forever.
Yes I must say, forever yes.
Never has such beautiful faith
swelled in me than now, never such
a sweet confession than this yes.
Say what you want. I believe you.

Hunter:

How easy you make this business
for me, for you, and this dear Queen.
For that, thanks. But believe me, girl,
I've been bold-faced lying to you.
For the sake of my mistress there,
I tell nothing but fairy tales.

Snow White:

No, no, don't tell lies to yourself.

I know that it's your soul that speaks.
I trust you. O, such confidence
is safe, has never trusted wrong.
Speak lies. My confidence makes them
into truth as pure as silver.
In fact, I can predict them all.
Whatever you think and say,
this yes will press truth on your words.
Speak, for me, ever faithful,
yes is this prisoner and longs
to be free of his stifling cell.

Hunter:

I speak then free of guilt and shame
here for the Queen. Do you believe?

Snow White:

Do I believe this? Yes, why should
I not believe in so much love?
I believe. Be off. I believe.
Just very happily be off.

Hunter:

That she drove me to this misdeed
with fiery kisses isn't true.
The fairy tale lies, which thus speaks.

Snow White:

How could it be true since you say
it's not. Be off, I believe.

Hunter:

That she hates you like a snake,
desirous of your sweet beauty
is a lie. She's a beauty too,
like a resplendent summer tree.
Behold her and call her lovely.

Snow White:

> Lovely, O how lovely. Spring's lush
> splendor is hardly so gorgeous.
> She surpasses in grandeur
> an image of polished marble
> when sculpted by a true artist.
> She is sweet like a gentle dream.
> The fancy of a fevered brow
> could not form such a fairy scene.
> And how can she be so jealous
> of me who stands like the winter
> at her side, so frosty and cold?
> I don't believe it. How could she?
> Go on then, you see, in this case,
> I am of the same mind as you.

Hunter:

> Beauty hates not beauty as much
> as a fairy tale has spread here.

Snow White:

> No, she's surely lovely herself.—
> So why hate this sister image,
> one who is begging at her feet
> and asks that, in the same shadow,
> it might exist in her imminence?

Hunter:

> That I wanted to kill you is
> an endless childish fantasy.
> I never had the heart for it.
> From the very start I was touched
> by this sad, sweet, childlike pleading
> spoken by both your mouth and eyes.
> I lowered my dagger and arm,
> lifted you up, my sweet, to me.

The deer, which had leapt in our way,
I stabbed myself. Isn't that so?

Snow White:

I hardly see it worth the time
to bear out this story. Why, yes,
of course. So it was. Yes, indeed.

Hunter:

The Queen never dispatched poison
intended for you to your dwarfs.
The poison apple isn't true.
The lie that says so is poison.
She herself who makes such claim has
ripened like a beautiful fruit,
tempting, full of flattering splendor,
but inside it would sicken who
is bold enough to taste it.

Snow White:

It's a lie, black and fantastic,
repugnant to hear, for scaring
children with. Be gone with this lie.
Are you kidding? I beg of you,
wring another stupid lie's neck
that just tries to be so clever.
Why is the Queen so quiet?

Hunter:

She contemplates vain misery.
She thinks of the mistake that plunged
you both in flames of vicious strife.
She weeps for so much confusion.
If I may ask, Snow White, kiss her,
something that would express some love.

Snow White (kisses her):

> Then permit me this sweet token.
> See how pale you are! Forgive me
> if I take your pallor's life with
> these kisses. See, they sponge it up,
> every bit of this tragic hue
> that would so disfigure your bliss.
> Hunter, have you nothing newer?

Hunter:

> O, still so much, but silence now.
> An end kisses in the end, though
> a beginning is still not through.
> The Queen gives me a gracious nod
> and my words choke up in her grace.
> As one blessed, I keep my silence.

> *The King, the Prince, ladies-in-waiting, and nobles appear.*

Snow White:

> O good Father, with your august
> seal press on that not yet smothered
> strife between these two burning hearts.
> Accept this kiss, and trample out
> this jealous strife into the ground
> as an emissary of peace.

King:

> I always thought you peaceable.
> What kind of strife, my lovely child?

Queen:

> No more strife, just a smiling word,
> a jest taking a serious mien
> that tricks you with a looming brow.
> There was some strife here, but no more.
> Love knew how to win here. Hate

36

perished in such a stronger love.
I did hate—it was just a game,
a tantrum taken much too far,
the bluster of a passing mood.
No more than that. Now it's sweet peace.
For a while a wounded envy
felt it had to hate. Ah, that hurt
myself more than anyone else.
Snow White here can affirm me.

King:

Is the Hunter blameless? The Prince
here bitterly accuses him.

Snow White:

Pureness points to heaven no more.
Perhaps you believe he trafficked
in illicit love with the Queen,
exchanging kiss and embrace, O,
don't believe that. You are deceived
by the temperament of this man,
which is as precious as a gem.
Love must cherish him, honor crown
him beyond doubt. Brave man, to whom
more gratitude than gratitude
can ever owe, I repay you.
(To the King) Lord, everything is peaceable,
and strife looks just like a blue sky.

King:

Here indeed then a miracle
has happened during this short hour.

Prince:

The villain is villain no more.

Queen:

> Hush, noble prince, it's ignoble,
> such a weakness for minor faults,
> in the scene you keep pointing at,
> whose flowering you sought after,
> shielding him instead. Were he great,
> we'd not now be standing gathered
> so peacefully. Give me your hand,
> forget the guilt in a friend's press.

Prince:

> I should forget that here is this
> confounded poisonous villain,
> the green knave in the hunting clothes,
> who for but a short hour courted
> such rich favor from the Queen?
> Make me forget that I am an
> anointed prince and a ruler,
> but not this sin, which is too great
> for just any oblivion.

Snow White:

> O, there's no longer any sin.
> It's no longer in this circle.
> It's fled from us. The sinner here,
> I, as her true child, kiss her hand
> and ask of her if she might but
> sin as much in so dear a way.
> Why, Prince, why do you stir up strife?
> Have you forgotten what you swore
> only but a short time ago?
> Did you not swear love to the Queen,
> kneel for her beautiful image
> of devotion and sweet splendor?
> Show now love, it truly befits

you best to joyfully render
the homage here of a shy kiss.
I, too, I thought I had been hurt,
the one harmed, hated, and cast out.
How stupid and stubborn I was
alike to see an evil sin,
to hastily trust in mistrust
and be so blind in bitterness.
Cast off the rash prejudice of
condemnation and fierce justice.
Justice is this clemency here,
and clemency is peace enwreathed,
part of this sweet, blessed revel
that tosses sin into the air,
plays with it as with the flowers.
Be happy you can be happy.
O, could I speak. I must too
for such a great and blessed end.
But I lack that gift for eloquence;
passion is much too wild in me
and I am so intensely filled
by such lofty, contrary joy.

Queen:

Oh, but how sweet you speak, fair child!

King:

Take this kiss, and may all have
a fete of royal joy this day.
Prince, you'd be better served if you
fell in with the general delight.
You don't want to be a stranger
and apart from such faithfully
devoted, heartfelt happiness.
What? Why do you still look angry?

Prince:

>Not angry, nor charming either.
>I just don't know what I should say.

Prince exits.

Queen (to Snow White):

>And are you no longer tired now?
>You want to laugh again, have fun,
>and spread cheer as if it were seed?

Snow White:

>I'm tired no more. What? Did the Prince
>run in fear from our rejoicing?
>Does this befit this noble man?

Queen:

>Sure it befits—he's a coward!

Snow White:

>I don't know if he's a coward.
>But such conduct's awful of him.
>Go, Hunter, bring him back here.

Hunter exits.

>I want to scold him when he comes,
>and he'll surely come. He just wants
>us anxiously seeking for him.

Queen:

>Then he will still be your sweetheart.
>And then—then I say, yes indeed,
>must say something I remember, say—
>What do I say? Ah, yes, then say,
>something like this perchance, saying:
>"You fired him on with your kisses
>to that—"

Snow White:
    Hush, O hush. Just the fairy tale
    says so, not you and never me.
    I said it just once, once like that—
    it's over and done. Father, come.
    Lead the way inside for us all.

                                    All go toward the castle.

THORN ROSE, THE SLEEPING BEAUTY

Thorn Rose:
> You, you who stand in this circle,
> please take a good look at this man.
> He woke me from my hundred years
> of deep sleep and so he wishes
> to now take me to be his wife.

King:
> He will wish he was not so bold.
> What has he done that's important?

Thorn Rose:
> He came by this way and kissed me,
> and with this kiss he woke me up.

First Lady-in-Waiting:
> Anybody could just as well.

Queen:
> Surely he has freed the castle
> and lifted the spell over us,
> yet that, I would hope, should hardly
> warrant such a desire as his.

King:
> I would hope too,

Second Lady-in-Waiting:
> me too,

Thorn Rose:
> me too.

King:

> Say, good stranger, could you give fair
> proof of exactly who you are too?

Thorn Rose:

> Does he not have eyes like the sea,
> a countenance like marble,
> and a deportment like granite?
> Well, I would not like such people.
> Let him find another sweetheart.

Third Lady-in-Waiting:

> Above all, should he not behave
> a little friendlier? He stands
> like a fence post and doesn't move.
> Nor has his mouth opened either.
> Hey? Can you say something or not?

Stranger:

> I will talk enough later on.
> There's really no terrible rush.

King:

> He awakened us from our sleep
> and seems quite still asleep himself.

Groundskeeper:

> This service that he has performed
> is rather doubtful and he could
> have easily spared himself
> all this trouble for our sake.
> Wasn't it lovely just to sleep?
> Were we not so much better off?

Coachman:

> If I still slept, I'd not have to climb

on my box now and be bothering
with those stubborn, stamping horses.

Cook:

If I still slept, I would not now
have to fight with the scullion maids.

Scullery Maid:

And I wouldn't have to pluck chickens,

Mamselle:*

and I wouldn't have to fluff the pillows,

Servant:

I would not have to shine these shoes.

Hunter:

The game would be asleep like me
had this monsieur here not come around.

Accountant:

The books would trouble me no more.
I never did settle accounts,
and balances never worried me.

Court Poet:

If I were asleep, no verses
would have to be labored over.
I'd still be lying on my ear
and dreaming of nothing but fame.
Now I'll wrestle around for rhymes,
earning nothing but ingratitude.
I would rather he had kept to
his cuckoo nest or somewhere else
that suited him and let us sleep.
This was no masterpiece on his part.

* A chambermaid.

Minister:

>If only I were still asleep.
>I would not be taxing my brain
>with such difficult alliances.

Governess:

>Must I warn the children all over
>to be on their best behavior now?
>Perhaps no one thinks of what a world
>of trouble this is going to cost me.

Professor:

>Science and scholarship for my sake
>could have still continued slumbering
>peacefully a little while longer.

First Lady-in-Waiting:

>Anyway, he surely claims credit
>for his having accomplished something.
>If only he had graced someone else
>with his presence sooner instead
>and had been willing to spare us it.

Thorn Rose:

>But there he is now after all.

King:

>Sadly, yes.

Thorn Rose:

>Say, how'd you get here?
>Don't you have eyes like the ocean?
>Did the waves toss you ashore here?
>Did you fall from the clouds to us?

Stranger:

>Did I come so undesired then?

Thorn Rose:
> So as to disturb my pleasant dream.

Stranger:
> Isn't reality a dream too?
> Aren't we all, even when awake,
> going about a bit like dreamers,
> sleepwalkers in the light of day,
> who play around with caprices
> and act as if awake?
> Well, we are, but what is being awake?
> Does some god lead us by the hand?
> Would he not do so where we have gone?
> Have we any guarantee that we
> would survive without someone higher?
> Could we persist without this support
> that we therefore do not apprehend,
> because it is a riddle to us?
> All is a dream, our houses are,
> trade, industry, our food each day,
> the cities, the countries and the
> light and the sun. No one can claim
> he understands. Understanding
> is but piecemeal, never otherwise.

King:
> Just give us details.

Stranger:
> As you know,
> I felt bored at my father's court.
> So one day I just wandered away
> to see for myself what they call life,
> and when I felt myself getting tired,
> I slept where I could on the hard ground,
> and afterward I walked once more,

and if someone stood in my way,
I fought for myself. Then I heard
about you.

Thorn Rose:

About me?

Stranger:

They said
you slept in a tower surrounded
by wild roses and thorns, that you
were under a spell. Only he who
broke through to you could rescue you.

Thorn Rose:

That whetted your curiosity.

Stranger:

Perhaps I felt like taking the risk.
I continued on my journey
without ever having seen you,
just you in spirit before me,
with me every step of the way.
At twilight, I would spend the time
thinking of how gentle you were and
sweet, and how wonderful it would be
to stir you, for me to look upon
you a little, to draw you toward me
tighter and tighter and you thinking
of me, that I am good enough.
Perhaps I stand here somewhat awkward.
However, something happens as I
just stand here in person, and I do.
So I wandered on and then came here,
walked without any long second thoughts
into this enveloping rankness,
which, like it knew the time had come,

pulled away its thorns then and there
such that I found unobstructed
an entrance and hastened to you.
I saw and kissed you. Then you opened
your eyes,

Thorn Rose:
                    because I had been surprised
by such a bold intruder?

Stranger:
                    Many,
of those who weren't as lucky as me,
I saw lying on the ground. A few
seemed to be smiling, as if they
were content in death to have achieved
this tempting prize.

Thorn Rose:
                    Those poor men, O those
valiant souls risking life with disdain,
to whom something seemed more beautiful,
to crumble away exemplary,
to have conquered both love and honor,
to exist less worthy and less brave.
I will think about this all my life
and the thought shall be bracing to me,
like a flower's fragrance. I would be
awful if I didn't think of it
continually as though it were
my own breath.

Stranger:
                    How true, how true, and I'm
plainly embarrassed at my success
to stand before you—

Thorn Rose:

                       —where so many
good men had to die, who fervently
desired me just as much as you,
who with blue-flashing eyes and blond hair,
with unsullied courage, with their young
breasts full of youthful compulsion
to snatch from life its zest, competed
for me—you alone touched what fate
would not grant them. We struggle
in vain when it won't, even when
giants take our cause. Lady Fortune!
Pooh! For a moment there, I was
almost becoming annoyed. Well look
now! I am beginning to believe
you have a right to me and it's the right thing
that I belong to you now.

Queen:

Don't you want to think this step through?
Think about what you're saying here.

Thorn Rose:

Were I to think it over longer,
I could spoil it for me in the end.
No, I am entirely in agreement
with myself, and he is my lord now.
Still, I would rather see my hero
otherwise, as one much more handsome,
somewhat more pleasing and elegant,
more charming too, and in a certain
sense prouder. But, alas, I cannot
say these things. I must accept him now, as
he is, and do so sincerely.

Stranger:

I am your gallant servant always!
And should I but only half please you,
should you have to all but force yourself
to see, to love, and to suffer me,
let me tell you a French proverb now:
L'appétit vient en mangeant.* I hope
that I shall succeed in pleasing you.

Thorn Rose:

So be it! Now let there be music
and let's all be happy together.
The sun is shining and the sky is
looking blue, and winds are fanning us
with uninhibitedly cool air.
This palace is now coming to life.
And going forward every one of us
will cheerfully challenge ourselves
and eagerly help where there is need,
with our eyes looking bright and living
happy as one and in such a way
that all things considered we shall build
toward a flourishing companionship.

King:

Because what you say, child, isn't bad,
count me in,

Queen:

me too,

Stranger:

and me too
because it can't happen otherwise.

* Appetite comes with the eating.

Thorn Rose:

>Me too, for clearly without me
>it does not happen.

Stranger:

>>No, it does not.

Thorn Rose:

>But it can happen—

Stranger:

>>—yes, yes, it can.

Thorn Rose:

>The longer we talk, the colder
>our soup gets, so let's break off here
>and together go to dinner.
>May I please have your arm?

Everyone:

>Thus the affair came to an end
>pleasantly and in wedded bliss.

CINDERELLA

A garden behind a house.

Cinderella:
    I will not cry so that they scream
at me for crying. My crying,
not their screaming, is what's awful.
When their hate doesn't make me cry,
the hate is good and sweet like cake.
It would be a jealous black cloud
blotting out the sun if I cried.
No, if I cried, I'd feel the hate
so hard it wouldn't be content
with mere tears. It would take my life,
a monster like that would eat me
dead. Its highly poisonous nature
is so lovely to me, the blithe
creature who never cries, who knows
no tears save only those of joy,
of only mindless happiness.
There is an imp inside my head
and he knows nothing of sadness.
Whenever they make me cry, there
cries this jolly sense inside me.
When they hate me, my joy loves them
that cannot even hate the hate.
When they come for me blind with rage,
with poison arrows of their wrath,
I smile like so. My presence shines
like the sun to theirs. Its bright ray
may not touch them, but in a flash
it will dazzle their wicked hearts.

And I, since I'm always occupied,
I really have no time for crying,
only laughter! Work laughs. Hands laugh.
They do. This soul laughs with a joy,
with what should win over the souls
of others no matter how stubborn.
Come heart, laugh my troubles away.

She wants to go. Her sister, in the window above.

First Sister:
That thing acts as if she were worth
looking at, standing there stock-still,
like a pillar in the sunlight,
splendor to the eye only she sees.
Get your lazy hide to the kitchen.
Do you no longer remember
your scant responsibilities?

Cinderella:
I'm going already, calm yourself.
Some reverie overwhelmed me
as I was on my way just now.
I was thinking of how pretty
you are, your darling sister too,
how you wear such pretty faces,
how it makes me more envious.
Forgive me and let me humbly
take my leave now.

She exits.

First Sister:
What a silly stupid dreamer.
We're way too soft on her. The fake
secretly laughs us off, pulling
her sad face when we surprise her

laughing at us behind our backs.
From now on, I'll give her the whip
for being so lazy on the sly.
That apron wraps her up in such
a dusty, black cloud. Then she dreams,
the hypocrite, who even now
stands idle. I will shortly go
and see that she gets back to work.

She closes the window.

Change of scene. A room in the royal palace.

Prince:

What makes me so melancholy?
Is my mind taking leave of me?
Is my life oppressed by remorse?
Is it in my nature to grieve?
Grief is sweet joy's adversary,
which I feel when I'm miserable.
But from where intrudes this sly shame
on my abandoned wits? Neither
wit nor its friend insight can tell.
I simply bear it in silence
while it weighs on me.—Ah, music!*
Whose voice sounds so serenely clear?
Whatever it is, I kiss it
kissing me so impossibly.
In this sweet kiss lies tranquil calm.
Grief has fled. I hear nothing more
than this sound. I feel nothing more
than this lovely dance's lesson
with my limbs. Could melancholy

* Cinderella's singing.

dance with so light a step? Well there,
it's flown out the door and I feel
wonderfully happy once more.
The Fool?

Fool:

It's the Fool indeed and ever
the fool, it's the fool of the realm,
the world's fool and that dear sweet fool
who'd be nothing if not foolish,
the paragon of foolery,
a fool on Monday and likewise
Saturday night, a fool all told,
a fool for himself and for his lord,
a right humble fool for his lord.

Prince:

Now tell me something, what is grief?

Fool:

It is a fool, and who admits
it himself is no less a fool.
That you are its fool I can tell
by that bittersweet face of yours.
Oy, even your youth calls you fool
and so happens the fool himself.

Prince:

Is there not a cause for my grief?

Fool:

You are its cause, the soil from which
it gaily blooms. You are the scales
on which it weighs itself, the bed
on which it lies stretched out. There is
no other reason save yourself.

Prince:

How then can I escape this grief
when I am such a pool of it,
what I would dare call: grief itself?

Fool:

Does a fool have to tell you this?
Should foolishness be so lofty,
may I ask, over the head of
a well-bred man? Why? Admit it,
this thing ill suits that wit of yours.

Prince:

I have whipped my wit, I flog it
like a tired lazy dog no more.
Now it's dead and it will never
wag its little tail anymore.

Fool:

I think it's right that we switch clothes.
You are a fool and as a fool
I take you by the ear. Next slap
yourself on the head, call yourself
stupid, and then you must stoop low
to my jokes that ridicule you.
Is this what you want? Have you had
enough of majesty—really?

Prince:

I'd be happy to give them up.
However, for your cap and bells,
I cannot exchange my burden
that I would gladly throw away.

Fool:

Go hunting. A spirited steed,
the exultant call of the horns—

such glories this pastime contains,
to slay the thing that you mean here,
inconsolable grief, that is.

Prince:

Very well, I take your counsel
no more, no less than my father
takes his from his wise chancellor
when his own wisdom seems lacking.
Come, follow me. I shall exit
this scene like an old-fashioned prince
in a classic play. Today, Fool,
you are a fool in the best sense.

He exits.

Fool:

By the devil, *that* I can believe,
and for me it would be easy.
It doesn't lack in flattery.
At heart, I am very flattered.
A prince well proves himself a fool
taking care not to be a fool.
I, who am not a prince, am lord
in the proper sense of the word,
for I am a master of wit.
My wit prevails over my lord,
who fell from his wit as my wit
raised him up to his princely state.
A prince with no fool is that wit
which will flop over and over.
I am buffoonery enthroned
above his station and scorning
a prince so in need of his fool.
And thus am I his fool indeed,

that I am for his foolishness.
Come, Fool, and let's follow the fool.

He exits.

Change of scene. An avalanche in the forest. The Prince on horseback.*

Prince:
> Down into the plain and raging,
> like a storm-swollen stream. Trees fall
> before the eyes. The heavens reel.
> The world's a joyous chase, a game
> preserve for noble hunters, whose
> minds range above earthly pursuits.
> What cheer I feel, what sweet pluck,
> how happy I am. This courage
> makes my heavy soul feel light,
> like a bird feels on the wing.
> Right now, I feel like a painting—
> lifeless, and yet so full of life,
> fully in control, yet excited,
> bitter and sweet. This carefree chase
> is, indeed, the very image
> of noble courage, which I serve now
> with all my heart while forgetting
> what's so heartfelt. The forest is
> my passion. It is my ballroom
> where arms and legs feel joyfully
> exercised. The trees are the rugs
> and pillows at my father's court.
> How wonderfully they wrap me.
> No dream could be more beautiful.

* An ironic play on teichoscopy, a classic dramatic device.

No picture sweeter than this art
a benevolent goddess painted herself.
Today was time spent like a warrior,
a moment so exquisitely fulfilled.
It's a joy that goes by all too soon.

Change of scene. A large room with a gallery connected by a flight of stairs. Cinderella and the First Sister.

Cinderella:

Look down at my devotion.
Look, look. O my every feeling
is ready to be at your service.
It is like a dress-shop box
opened to show a gift within,
like a new fur to keep you warm.
O how warmly my heart serves you.
I beg you, boldly strike my hand
if even for a second I don't
toe the line with the bat of your eye.
But this can never be for my one,
my sweetest joy is to serve you.

First Sister:

You stupid kitchen wench, not worth
the flogging you'd get from the whip.

Cinderella:

I'm always at your feet. I could
kiss your hand, that gentle hand,
the one that never strikes me
save for rightful punishment.
With your eyes, you regard me
like the sun. And I am the soil
that thrives on its merciful kiss,
on which nothing else ever can

as it lovingly blooms to you.
But, alas, loving I am not.
Indeed, I am devoid of love—
only my sister is the fairest,
yet not so beautiful as kind.
She is prettier than kindness.
What joy there to be at her feet,
devoted, to be her servant.

First Sister:

Stop prattling so much. The time spent
talking could be spent doing some work,
to put forth devoted effort.
Now take your hand off my dress!

Cinderella:

If I must serve devotedly
and I mustn't require a hand,
with what shall I do my work?
Would it only get done in thoughts
on the fly, then this filthy hand
that angers you won't be required.
My yearning would put your clothes on,
wait on you with the finest things.
Then my heart would be a servant,
one just gentle enough, perhaps.
So a joy for work works for you—
wouldn't that surely work for you?

First Sister:

Would you shut up for once. And who
likes hearing all this chatter too.

Cinderella:

And who would—indeed—and my tongue
must work in a hurry with my hand

so that happiness keeps them both
out of breath. This way when a word
pops out of my mouth and would tempt
my hand, when such lures from the tongue
its abundance, my merry words
soon double what hands can do, like
words with fingers. Hand and voice kiss,
both married in the dearest way.

First Sister:

Both of them are lazy. And you,
their mistress, are as well. That's why
you must always get a beating.
Off with you now.

She exits.

Cinderella (calling to her):

Beat me, beat me.

The Prince appears above in the gallery.

Prince:

I don't know how I came into
this fairy tale. I only asked
for a drink the way hunters do.
However, these rooms here are such
eyes can't see, the mind not easily
grasp. A glow floats upon the wall.
The scent of yellow roses spreads forth.
Like a soul it comes and goes
and solemnly takes my hand.
I stand still as if enchanted.
This thing clings to my senses.
Then this narrow space reopens.
The roof sways. This gallery dances
softly underfoot. What's going on?

Ah, below is some sweet presence.
I will accept what this thing is
even if I can't understand it.

Cinderella:

Whichever way I spin round
makes me act the wrong way.
This heart's a ball in play!
And, like little balls, feelings roll
this way and that just for fun.
I, who should stop them,
am the object of this game.
This scares me, but at the same time
I have so little to worry about.
I laugh, but in my laughter
something's serious, ominous,
which makes me laugh anew.
The seriousness it gives my work
is such frightful fun it would make
even bitter fate smile, which, I think,
isn't easy. No, when I cried
my cares and troubles laughed at me.
I'd rather laugh them both away
into a dear and touching thing.
There's still plenty of time left
to cry once time itself cries.

Prince (leaning over the railing):

Are you a fairy tale, fair child?
Are your feet and hands such
that if I touched them their beauty
would disappear into thin air?
I beg of you as one who pleads
for mercy. Are you an image
and only appear as such?

Cinderella:

>Sir! I am Cinderella.
>See the dirt on my dress? It says so
>as clear as does my mouth.

Prince:

>You're an angel. Tenderness,
>as if embarrassed by that word's
>meaning, stammers you're an angel.
>What else could you be?

Cinderella:

>A silly little thing
>properly embarrassed,
>who'd like to know who you are.

Prince:

>You give and receive my answer
>at the very moment you ask.

Cinderella:

>No, don't tell me. You're a prince,
>a king's son. I can see that
>in this lost creature who no longer
>fits in our time. An ermine cape
>is draped over your shoulders.
>You carry a sword and lance
>no longer in style. That's what I see.
>But I could be mistaken.
>A king's son, you are surely.

Prince:

>Surely, just as you are to me
>a bride.

Cinderella:

>Did you say that I am your bride?
>O don't say that! It hurts me to see

myself mocked and so tenderly misloved
by such a well-meaning young man.

Prince:

I can already see a crown
shimmering, pressed into your hair,
an image before which art stands
aloof and love looks at a loss.

Cinderella:

Why did you come here then and how?

Prince:

This the fairy tale tells you last,
when on the dear fairy tale's lips
this silence lies, when voice and sound,
color and noise, and waterfall
and lake and forest have faded.
When this happens, at once just how
will spring into your eyes. But then
why I am here I do not know.
Pity and tenderness are sly
spirits, indeed, whose work cannot
be divined. So simply be still.
Submit yourself to the stern fate
that has befallen you. It will
all come to an explanation.

Cinderella falls into contemplative sleep.

The King and Chancellor appear above in the gallery.

King:

Look, we have snared the griffin bird.*
Now have I got my claws on you,

* A mildly pejorative expression in the German, compare to a "rare"
or "strange bird."

you rascal, you good-for-nothing.
Seeing it's my son angers me.

Prince:

Hush, Father, don't trouble yourself.

King:

I am not troubled by this son,
who stands there like a red-faced boy
at my reproach. Are you facing
some knave, me who came upon you,
that you dare speak in such a way?
Explain to the high crown right now
how you came here, right here, here and
now. Spit it out! Hey! Will I get
that stammering confession soon,
running circles around my ears?

Prince:

I neither wear a red face, nor
would I stammer as you believe.
Calm yourself down, Father, be still.
I have an announcement to make,
to you, the realm, the world. I am
engaged.

King:

How so?

Prince:

Yes, yes, engaged in every sense,
as one's words can only convey,
a vow to pledge, so I'm engaged.

King:

Well! To whom?

Prince:

To a miracle who will not
be a miracle. A creature
such that only a girl can be,
but yet like a girl unheard of.
An image before which magic
takes a knee and rubs its blind eyes.
The divine is in the picture,
so it moves, has life, and belongs
to me as I to it. It's a bond,
my father, not to be broken.
Blood was shared, and in ours no one
will see the sweetest love end.

King:

Come, Chancellor, come!

Prince:

Allow me to kiss your hand, let
love fall down and beg at your feet.
She's the one I want to be mine,
who's worth the throne in every sense.
She will be an embellishment
to our dynasty, a sweet joy
in old age. O chase this sunlight
not from the snow of your white head!
This girl you will warm to, and she'll
enchant you as she enchants me.

King:

Silence, you have no idea
what I think where it concerns you.
Listen up, my son, I can wear
the face of a bull and I would
rather not have you on my horns.

Step aside, here in the black, so
we can have a word in the dark,
quietly resolve our discord.

Prince:
Don't you want to see her?

King:
I came with her in my mind's eye,
already caught up in this dream.
I feel quite well disposed toward her,
but don't take this to mean that now
I'm no longer opposed to you.
Step to the side here and you will
learn my fatherly intentions.

> *They step back into the gallery so that only their heads*
> *can be seen.*

Cinderella (upon awaking):
Now I would love to know if I
can feel around with these hands.
If it's a dream, there is nothing.
For dreams, even if they please us,
they just aren't worth getting up for.
I want to move this foot—like so—
and now this hand, and now the head.
The gallery above, from which
that sweet man leaned over to me,
is really and truly there, though
I don't remember and can't ask
how a prince came to bow to me.
Be what it will, this thing is not
so quick to be utterly doomed.
Maybe it never happened then.

I only just dreamt about it
in a dream while falling asleep.
But this head and that smile happened
as if in some reality
that was mine before sleep. Sleep has
made me mistrustful and timid.
It has ruined the game in which
I was so blissfully forlorn.
Now I'll take a few steps and see
if I can still walk. My eyes go
around in a circle and see
everything spic-and-span, indeed
mysterious not in the least,
as I had wanted it. Well, this has,
everything thus far said, has time.
The sisters come.

Both sisters enter.

First Sister:
Hey, Cinderella!

Second Sister:
"Here," she will say. "I'll be right there."
That will be her sorry excuse.

Cinderella:
Don't be angry for I'm here now.
On my knees if you so desire,
kissing you hand and foot. Never
have I been so quick and ready
to serve, so happy to obey.
Please tell me what I am to do.

Second Sister:
Tie up the shoe here on my foot.

First Sister:

Go to the shoemaker for me.

Cinderella:

I will gladly jump for you soon,
but there's a tie that binds me here.
And when I'm so bound, my zeal flies
away for the sister who makes
me go. Then upon my return,
only weariness shall stand
in my place to serve you anew.
You will never see me weary
so long as you don't allow it.

Second Sister:

That is really laced up too tight,
you lazy clod, here! Take that!

She pushes her away.

First Sister:

Leave, make off with you, and don't you
dawdle on the streets and corners.

Cinderella exits.

Prince (in the gallery):

Doesn't that vain pair of sisters
brood there like hate and resentment?
How slender they are—beautiful
if their natures were not ravaged
by ignorance, livid envy.
Yes, like sinister clouds, they blow
around this sweet, sunny image,
their little sister, who is wholly
intimidated by their power
and no more knows to help herself.

This ought to be a fairy tale
for children—and grown-ups as well—
the two towers of fashion there
and their little deer they despise,
despised for being so beautiful.
Where would it flee? It's fit to make
the leap only too well, I think.
That it flee from me I dread always.
Hey there, you sisters!

First Sister (looking around):
    What does this big brute want?

Second Sister:
    Look you, you are too crude for us.
    Go about your nasty business,
    rouse your dogs, clutch your big skewer,
    go shoot a rabbit to death. Here's
    no place for such an ill-bred boy.

Prince:
    Yes, indeed, all is good!

First Sister:
    Leave the fool to himself, sister.
            They speak to each other. Cinderella enters unnoticed.

Prince (softly):
    You nightingale, you lovely dream,
    you, above every fantasy,
    a sublime apparition, see
    how quick my hands come together
    in their veneration of you.
    The language must be a weasel
    falling headlong when it wishes
    that it didn't lack words for her,

but it can see her poverty.
The wonder of her seals its lips:
in this way does love hold its breath.

Cinderella (smiling):
Hush—you throat-clearer—hush!*

Prince:
My father desires to see you
on his lap as his crowned child.

Cinderella:
Is he an older man? Is he
the country's king?

Prince:
Yes, indeed he is. I'm his son.
Just now he called me a rascal,
who leads him around by his big nose.
Now he's smiling and shedding tears
that stream down his big round full cheeks.
But when I asked him why he cried,
suddenly I'm a rapscallion,
a man ignorant of honor,
a thief of supreme majesty,
a perfect criminal. So I
keep quiet, quiet as a mouse,
and do not disturb his sleep
while he dreams of your elegance.

Cinderella:
And if he does, will he not still
admit being a rascal to you?

Prince:
Absolutely.

* Directed at the Prince, who cannot hold his breath.

Cinderella:
> Now hide yourself.

The Prince returns to his previous position.

Cinderella:
> Laugh quietly my angels, who
> hover in the air around me;
> they point out at the heads up there,
> the ones above this gallery,
> which are somewhat half visible.
> Just look at that gigantic crown
> that deserves such a hearty laugh.
> Look at that knotted knitted brow.
> Now behold the head of a youth
> and think hard about who it is;
> the Prince, assuredly, it is not.
> His head perhaps, but it's not, too;
> because surely a half a head
> cannot be taken for the head.
> The nice thing about this charade
> is that you must laugh in silence,
> quite softly so that no one hears,
> especially not my sisters,
> who exist apart from laughter,
> who would be taken aback, and
> yet don't feel it. Indeed, there is
> someone sleeping in the great hall.
> It's as if empathy were packed
> in a matchbox. I am tired too
> from putting all this into words.
> This gallery column right here
> will do as my little cradle.

She leans on a column.

Fairy Tale, fantastically garbed, appears from behind the Prince's and
the King's back.

Fairy Tale (whispering):
    Cinderella!

Cinderella (stepping forward):
    Well, now what's this? Who are you? Speak!

Fairy Tale:
    I am Fairy Tale, from whose lips
    everything spoken here resounds,
    from whose hand these images' charm,
    which here enchant, take flight, and go,
    that can wake your feelings of love
    with sweet gifts intended for you.
    Observe, these dresses will make you
    the most beautiful young lady,
    place the hand of the Prince in yours.
    Look at the way this one sparkles,
    how this one flashes. Precious stones,
    pearls, corals readily desire
    to adorn your breast, to fetter
    gracefully neck and arm. Take them,
    and do take it, the entire outfit.

                              She lets the dress fall to the ground.
    If it should feel too tight on you,
    don't worry, an elegant dress
    presses itself tight to one's limbs,
    eagerly fitting the body.
    Now, let us move on to the shoes.
    I believe that you have small feet,
    very petite, the kind he likes.
    Won't you be wanting shoes as well?

                                      She holds them up high.

Cinderella:
> You're blinding me.

Fairy Tale:
> I came here to put fear in you.
> The people don't believe in me,
> but so what when just my nearness
> makes them think a little again.
> These shoes are silver but as light
> as swan's down. I simply ask you
> to hold them nimbly in your hands.
> > *She throws them into Cinderella's hands.*

Cinderella:
> Oh!

Fairy Tale:
> Don't taunt your sisters with them.
> Be noble with such noble splendor
> while comporting yourself just so,
> as your nature obligates you.

Cinderella:
> O, I promise you.

Fairy Tale:
> You are a dear, sweet child worthy
> of this fairy tale. Do not kneel!
> I beg you, if I am dear to you,
> kneel for her, whom I kneel before.

Cinderella (kneeling):
> No, let me. Gratefulness surely
> feels itself divinely enriched.

Fairy Tale:
> It is due to your mother that
> I come to you. Such a woman

as lovely as her lives no more,
ornamented by such virtue
that virtue was made lovelier
than her, the loveliest—alive
no longer save, perhaps, in you.
You have what's sweetest about her,
something that makes women divine,
this alluring serenity
which exists in a noble mind,
this inexpressible something
before which brave men kneel. Be still.
Put on that dress now in silence.
Slip into the palace tonight.
You know the rest of the story.
It's been dreamt long enough. This scene
must come to life now. To wonder
shall bring fear. And the fairy tale
goes on until its end, its home.

She exits.

Cinderella:

Now quick, lest the sisters catch me
too soon and suffer my lost time
too late. Some whim would rather still
linger here, but a lucky girl
can no longer marry a knave,
she who must flee with her rich things,
hide them. Some whim would rather still
smile here, and yet this happiness,
this smiling, is laughing me onward.
Hurry, lest the Prince see me like this!

She exits.

Prince:

  Hey, Cinderella!

King:

  The night has come, let us go home.

Prince:

  I must be here forever.

                          Three girls dressed as pages appear.

First Page:

  How funny I feel in these clothes.
  They have made me look like a boy.

Second Page:

  Mine tingles. It snags. It itches.
  It's an unnameable feeling.
  It kisses my entire body.

First Page:

  As I pulled them on over me,
  a fire blasted me in the face.
  I wear them now, but I don't know
  how I will ever keep them on.

Third Page:

  I feel like doing what boys will do.
  I want to jump, to laugh, to twirl
  my arms and my legs to and fro
  and yet I can't. Like a sin they
  are squeezing my fair young body,
  they are causing me to grow stiff.

First Page:

  But not even for a kingdom
  would I not love to feel such fear.

To me they hurt so well and so
pleasurably at the same time.

Second Page:
When the heavens and the earth lay
one atop the other, they'd feel
half so tightly pressed together
compared to this attire and me.

First Page:
Girls, the Prince calls.

Prince:
What do you want? Why are you here?

First Page:
To grace the scene the way your dream
and the fairy tale desire it.
For decoration we have draped
the gallery in precious cloth.
Now we'll spray perfume everywhere
to fill the room with its scent.
Now we'll light the candelabra
and make the night as bright as day.
If you still have further orders,
tell us.

Second Page:
Shall we assemble the people
to applaud this celebration?

Prince:
No, it's not that kind of party,
not what you think, needing people,
one that is framed by their shouting.
We'll have a party with ourselves,
a totally silent party,
where the public voice gets nothing

to trumpet and the world nothing
to concern itself. Heedlessness
celebrates here, a festive mood
filling our hearts, without worry.
Nor would we make much of a crowd
for any bothersome fellow,
since we would have no need of pomp
or vain splendor, which here never
has to see to our happiness.
I feel such silent happiness,
such a sweet and holy feeling,
that to think about a party
feels reprehensible to me.
I already felt festive here,
even before you brought candles
to light the feast. An anxious joy,
who's half ashamed and half happy,
who's an untold bundle of nerves,
who doubts in her success, she is
the party-giver here.

Third Page:

 Just this slender column's to do,
 my lord, spinning me like a bride.

Prince:

 Now do me this favor and leave.
 For your service, accept my thanks.

First Page:

 These are well-bred pages, taking
 leave when there is no longer need.

Second Page:

 Come away. This Prince's page is
 only a dream.

The pages exit.

Prince:

> I conduct myself in a dream
> so much now, I can handily
> submit to a foreign power.
> Is what I see before my eyes
> my possession? Am I indeed
> not set up as though in a game?
> Haven't I sat here long enough,
> while nothing will move me forward?
> I really think I am going mad
> and all this, what is around me,
> seems no less through the agency
> of magic. However, as said,
> I want domination, shackles.
> My blood, although it is princely,
> feels very well under such bonds,
> more than well. I would love to shout,
> I'd love to shout with such a voice
> that the echo would fade away
> above the whole world. O how nice
> bondage is here that otherwise
> darkens the place in which it reigns.
> I have never felt so anxious
> for the miraculous image
> that comes when the story's over.
> The end of this thing here must be
> a miracle, for it makes me
> suffer to wait so. Hey, Father!

King:

> This is getting painful. Come home.

Prince:

> My home will be forever here.
> I feel every single moment
> like a kiss. The passage of time

touches my cheeks caressingly,
my senses draw toward this perfume.
I will cling to this world here
as she to me. I will not come
away, not ever.

King:

And what if I order you now?

Prince:

You've neither say nor power here.
I give myself the final word.
I confer the power on me
that says not to listen to you.
Forgive me, Father, in me is
a rebellious, youthful impulse,
one you had too when you were young.
I'll stay and wait here till life stirs.

King:

Well must I too. But this hand has
yet to be extended, has yet
to forgive you for your speech.

Prince:

It is so infinitely dear
to forgive, so sweet to the one
who does so over and over.
That you'd likely forgive me
I knew for certain.

King:

What blather!

Prince:

I will forget that this strikes me
as very strange, so that even
anticipation keeps silent

and her conduct is still concealed
by a question. Yes, I am here
in a place so well beloved
that I can perhaps be patient.
But I am bothered by one thought:
Just where is Cinderella now?
Eh? What if she doesn't return?
What if she totally forgot
just where her empathy belongs?
This is improbable but not
unlikely. That which is likely
is a wide world, and that a thing
happened was already likely,
even while seeming unlikely,
is almost beyond my grasp too.
And what is likely beyond me
is still as good as being likely.
So be it. I will get a grip
on myself. It befits someone,
especially men, to be proud.
But what is the fear in pride then,
what affects it so? And such pride,
what could it be worth to yourself?
No, I wish to weep, that this child
far from me so long has a chance.
I want to think that only this
will ever be.

King:

    I fear while I stand here idle,
    my state totters. Let it sink
    into chaos. The fairy tale
    draws to an end and tickles
    my fancy; afterward will I
    be the divine order once more.
    Government enjoys its sleep too,

and the father of the law is
only human.

Prince:

I would willingly hold my breath
to hear her step all the better.
Yet she has such a light footstep
that even this inkling can't tell
when she approaches. O, she draws
near, here to this impatient sense,
whose muscles tear themselves apart
to feel her near. The way being near
can be so sweet when it concerns
the lover, and how brutal she is
when something bad intrudes on us.
Here only something lovely should
really be intruding, and yet
this is never the way of love.
She's silent where she must forget;
she doesn't have this loud echo
that signals falsehood. O, she is
rich, and words aren't necessary
to remember her by; surely,
O surely this dearest creature
cannot be far. My feeling says
this with spirit. Just the patience
to not evade who bides her time
is the one thing I think about.
I must stand here, standing as firm
as if some word could order me.
Lovers happily wait. To dream
of the beloved makes time fly.
What is time but just a quarrel
of impatience now becalmed?
What's that shining there upon me?

He comes down from the gallery.

King:
> I don't know what is the matter,
> why I'm married to silence here.
> I'm too old for marriage. Reason
> scolds me, points its finger at me,
> laughing out loud, but what's so wrong?
> Of course I'm old and have a right
> to be foolish. The indulgence
> goes very sprightly with white hair
> in general. I indulge my son
> to play the guardian bravely.
> Out of caprice, which at my age,
> you know, limps behind. I'll drop it,
> as the spirit of youth would want.
> I'm falling asleep—fatigue sits
> well in my silver hair, like sleep
> to a mind old and head-shaking.

Prince (below, with a shoe in his hand):
> I see this thing as a portent
> to approaching glory and love.
> It's a shoe for a shapely foot.
> It speaks of a pleasing nature
> as if it had a mouth, a gift
> for eloquence. And these fine jewels
> do not belong to her sisters,
> who have turned to stone over there.
> Where would they get such a foot too,
> so narrowly shaped for this shoe?
> Just whom could it belong to then?
> I don't want to face this question.
> It scares me. Could it really be?
> Does it belong to the girl? No,
> I torture myself needlessly.
> Who would give her silver and gold,
> who would give her such royal jewels?

And yet some inkling speaks to me
of Cinderella, which reveals
her strange behavior, her distance,
her style. Magic, as I well know,
is a possibility here.
I want to want it, for I can't
hold it, cannot get a grasp.

He climbs up the staircase reflectively, stalking Cinderella above
in a maid's dress, carrying the Fairy Tale's gifts in her arms.

Cinderella:

Could you still be here yet, my Prince?

Prince:

I am still here, my charming child,
only to behold you once more.
What have you there?

Cinderella:

See, it's a beautiful dress! Look
greedily at this majesty.
Such would bring joy to a king's eye.

Prince:

Who gave you that?

Cinderella:

O that wouldn't interest you much.
I don't even know exactly.
It's enough this sweet thing is mine
and that I can put it on now
if I wanted to. But—

Prince:

But—

Cinderella:

I no more do.

Prince:

>What has made you so strangely cold?
>Who clouded the lake of your soul
>with silt, so that it looks so dark?

Cinderella:

>I myself, and so just be still,
>please put aside your noble wrath.
>There will be no more hurting here.
>Only—

Prince:

>What? Tell me, love!

Cinderella:

>Only that something still pains me:
>among all these lovely things here
>something is still missing. I must be
>missing the left shoe—ah, that's it,
>that's it, of course.

Prince:

>Well, of course—and is this one yours?

Cinderella:

>How can you ask? It is just like
>its brother here on the table.
>So then I have this splendid gift
>in full, and so I can go forth.

Prince:

>Wearing that around your body,
>right, that around your fair body?

Cinderella:

>No, don't!

Prince:

>What's gotten into you suddenly?

Cinderella:

So suddenly—what is it then?

Prince:

That you don't love me anymore?

Cinderella:

I don't know whether I love you.
Yet again it's clear I love you,
for what kind of girl would not love
the high station and manliness,
the nobility, the fine cast?
I love your majesty that is
so patient and awaits my own.
I am touched that you, you alone
have shown such compassion for me.
Something touches me to the quick.
I'm nervous all of a sudden.
I stand utterly, miserably
exposed here. The least little breeze
will blow my heart into a storm,
to be so still soon afterward,
the same way it lies outspread now,
just like a peaceful, sunlit lake.

Prince:

Does your heart really feel like this?

Cinderella:

Like this and different. What one word
might express. Our language sounds
far too crude for expressing this.
Music is required to better
say this over and over. It,
it is playing.

Music.

Prince:

>Listen, what lovely dance music.
>Desire rises, swells inside me,
>and I can no longer bear it,
>that we stand here ever longer,
>dithering. Come, let me lead you
>in dance. Our ball begins here now,
>with our own magic power. Drop
>that silver-heavy burden, come.

Cinderella:

>In this dress, my lord, full of filth
>and covered with stains? So you want
>to dance with a kitchen apron,
>hold on tight to its soot and dust?
>I would be thinking otherwise,
>before I did such a thing.

Prince:

>Not me.

>>>*He carries her down the steps. When he is below:*
>A princely pair dances.

>>>*They dance. After a few rounds, the music stops.*

Cinderella:

>Look, look!

Prince:

>Like it's telling us to be still.

Cinderella:

>It wants this too. It's a very
>sensitive creature, not wanting
>its sound to be lost in the dance.
>It proves our imagination

is alive: we dance in a dream
as well as if it were real. In this case
a dance doesn't want to be danced,
to make noise. Empathy can dance,
too without foot and without sound.
Quiet, for we must listen, it's
what the music wants of us too!

The music begins anew.

Prince:

Listen, as sweet as any dream.

Cinderella:

Yes, it is a dream, so subtly
causing the dream to stir in us.
O, how it can't bear a wide room.
It escapes into the silence,
where it moves nothing but the air
slowly back and forth. Let us sink
completely into its substance.
Thereafter we will forget what
we must forget. Let us seek out
the trail that leads to empathy,
the one we lost in our vulgar
passions. It will not be easy
to find this sweetness. It requires
infinite patience, like a sense
rarely achieved. It's so easy,
like when we wish to comprehend
the incomprehensible. Come,
let's rest serene.

Prince:

Your words ring as sweet as music.

Cinderella:

> Hush, don't disturb me in this thought
> that, half resolved, gives me such pain.
> Once it gets out, I'll be happy
> and cheerful, as you prefer me.
> But it will never leave its cell,
> this sense of being forsaken, which
> I feel rising up in my heart.
> It will fade away like a sound,
> faint, guilty; and the memory
> will never die. A part remains
> with me until, perchance, there comes
> some freak thing to save me from it.

Prince:

> So what is this thought of yours then?

Cinderella:

> Nothing, nothing at all—a whim.
> When we hang on to a scruple
> for much too long—something stupid—
> yet that provides us with no end,
> since a beginning, middle, end
> are all but shifting things, never
> with any sense, never, ever
> knowing one's heart. The end is:
> I will be happy with you now.

Prince:

> How you move me, and how you charm
> me with your impulsivity,
> which, with every indication,
> has this noble bearing. We will
> forget who and just what we are,
> share happiness, like the anguish
> we sincerely shared. You're quiet?

Cinderella:

>Rather the captured nightingale,
>one who sits trembling in the snare,
>forgetting the song she would sing.

Prince:

>You sweet-talk me!

Cinderella:

>I'm all yours, so frightfully yours
>that you must lend me your body
>to hide myself deep inside it.

Prince:

>I shall offer you a kingdom—

Cinderella:

>No, no!

Prince:

>—a villa, in which you will dwell.
>It is tucked deep in a garden.
>Your view will come to rest on trees,
>on flowers, the dense greenery,
>on ivy garlanding the wall,
>on a sky that sends you sunlight
>more gorgeous than any other
>as it pierces chinks in the leaves.
>Moonlight there is more sensitive,
>the tips of the pine trees tickle
>it raw and tender. The birdsong
>is to your ears a recital
>inexpressibly beautiful.
>As its mistress you will wander
>through the art of the garden,
>upon paths that, as though they had
>empathy, part ways and rejoin

suddenly. Fountains brighten you,
the dreamer, whenever you dwell
in your thoughts too much. All of this
will come running to wait on you
and simply when it pleases you,
all feeling according to you,
all cheerfully subservient.

Cinderella:
You are teasing me. Isn't it,
isn't it true that I would feel
myself borne by hands? By your hand,
there is no doubt I'd be clinging
utterly and blissfully so.
But these dresses, which you see here,
I'm terribly in love with them.
I would have to put them aside,
no more to be Cinderella—

Prince:
Then you will have handmaidens and
wardrobes full of gorgeous dresses.

Cinderella:
Don't I have that?

Prince:
All day long in silence you would
be left to yourself. Only when
desire drove you from the garden
to people and to greater noise,
as it met your stillness, would you
find in the palace murmuring
enough delight, glitter, splendor,
music, dance, frolic, what you will.

Cinderella:

>This again would make for something
>like a very pleasant and lovely
>contrast to my solitude then.
>Do you think so?

Prince:

>Of course.

Cinderella:

>How I love you. I cannot find,
>in that wide, open, infinite
>land of gratitude, one small word
>to thank you. So let me, in place
>of every way to express thanks,
>kiss you, like so. O that was sweet.
>Good, now that it is at an end.

Prince:

>An end? To what?

Cinderella:

>This leaping comes to an end now,
>this dance with me. I'm not for you.
>I am still engaged to myself.
>Memory reminds me I've not
>yet dreamed this love through to the end,
>that something floats around me here,
>something here, something that gives me
>still much more to do. Don't you see
>the quiet sisters over there,
>hard as stone, watching us amazed?
>I feel sorry for them, although
>they're not worth feeling sorry for.
>But that is not being true, it is
>only said for my sake really.

I love them, who worked me so hard
and stern. I love the punishment
that was undeserved, those foul words,
so as to keep smiling brightly.
I get endless satisfaction.
It occupies me all day long,
gives me cause to leap and to see,
to think and to dream. And that is
the reason I am such a dreamer.
I was betrothed to you too soon.
You deserve someone better.
The fairy tale never tells this.

Prince:

The fairy tale wants it. It's clear,
the fairy tale will see us wed.

Cinderella:

A wide-awake fairy tale is
inside this dreaming creature here.
And I couldn't dream at your side!

Prince:

But, but—!

Cinderella:

No, not where I would be displayed
like I was a bird in a cage.
I couldn't take that, not being able
to kiss.

Prince:

But if you want to see it fly,
should you not expend some effort
to chase after it? You only dream
when you have to catch a dream.

Cinderella:

How nice you understand me. True,
so true.

Prince:

Now, now, compose yourself. I know
you're now going to put this dress on
that the fairy tale chose for you.
You were born to have such sweet things
and you can't escape these fetters,
these ten thousand too many whims
that all rise up inside of you.
May I conduct you toward the door?

They stand up.

See, it would be a shame for you.
This fineness you have inside you
ordains that you will be my wife.
You cry?

Cinderella:

For I must follow you despite
the aforesaid and so gladly
will I follow you from now on.

Prince:

I ask very, very much.

Cinderella gathers up the dresses and exits.

Hey, Father!

King (from above):

What kind of a girl is that, son?

Prince:

Is she good enough now?

King:

>As a goddess she shall ascend
>to my throne. Her ennoblement
>shall stir the land into music
>and revelry. I'll be right down
>and proclaim it to our nation.
>In the meantime she'll come with you
>amid rejoicing, which like incense
>will lead, follow.

>*He exits.*

Prince:

>I'll wait here until her return.

>>*To Cinderella, who appears above in the gallery in her*
>>*extravagant dress.*

>Ah, is it you?

Cinderella:

>To serve you, lord.

Prince:

>O dear, no! O how———

>>*He leaps up the stairs toward her.*

Cinderella:

>Yes, yes.

THE CHRIST CHILD

Joseph:
    What goes on inside this cottage?
    Who are these strange people I see?
    What a curious gathering!
    In the weak glow of my lantern,
    I can make out all kinds of faces.
    Who are you? Where do you come from
    and what would make you turn out here?
    Speak!

Young Girl:
        I can hardly explain why.
    I'd rather you didn't ask me.
    I only heard that here on this night
    something glorious would happen
    and thought I'd like to be here too,
    even though I am but a poor,
    scorned girl.

Soldier:
        Did they not say,
    the Long-Awaited One would be born?

Old Man:
    I heard something to that effect too.

Joseph:
    Who says so?

Soldier:
        I don't know.

Young Girl:
           Nor do I.

Joseph:

> But who are these worthy gentlemen
> in discussion among themselves?
> They appear to be of a high rank,
> as shown by their sumptuous garments.
> All this cultured bearing of theirs
> is too plain for me to take them
> to be mere humble folk.

First King:

> We are
> potentates from the Orient.
> Some give us the title of wise men.
> To others we appear as kings.

Joseph:

> Is that so? Well, that's fine by me.
> It's a shame that I can't wait on you
> with something.

Second King:

> We thank you from our hearts,
> but we don't need anything at all.
> Our being here is refreshment enough.

Joseph:

> Is it possible that you made
> such a long journey just to come
> and meet a simple carpenter?
> I can hardly understand why.
> Take no offense on my account.

Third King:

> It may well indeed have been God
> who gave us a sign to follow,
> to come here, inside this cramped space,

where lies that little boy, the one
who shall one day redeem mankind.

Joseph:

How did you come by this wonderful
idea? I'm almost frightened.
Of course, a child has been born here,
but hardly for such a lofty
purpose.

Soldier:

Show it to us.

Joseph:

If you would
like to see it now, take a quick look
around. It lies there in the corner
by his mother.—And you, boy, you're
in awe too?

Jester:

Incredibly so!

Vagabond:

I too would very much like to see
this miracle child.

Joseph:

Your glimpse is
granted you. Come, closer.

All step toward the child.

This is it!

Mary:

Who're these people you're talking to?

Joseph:

They would like to see our baby.
They say—

Mary:

Well, what do they say then?

Joseph:

It's the Messiah.

Mary:

What? This child?

Joseph:

Yes, and it be born for the sake
of the happiness of mankind.

Mary:

Have they been taken in by fraud?

Joseph:

To be honest, they just don't make
that impression on me, after all
they are too polite, they speak much
too thoughtfully. Talk to them yourself.

Mary:

You're most welcome. Thank you so much
for your company and kind faces,
and for being nice enough to have
asked us.

Shepherd:

Room for one or two more
might be found in this cubbyhole.

Joseph:

This crowd is getting rather large.
But I shall not bar you entry.

Instead, let me wish you a warm
good evening and ask that you make
yourselves at home as best you can.

Shepherd:
Outside all was silent, but for
singing from the starry sky: "Christ is
risen!" I thought I must see him
and now I realize this is it.

Soldier:
It's him.

Joseph:
      You have such perfect faith,
I might end up being a believer
myself.

Mary:
      Aren't you always a child,
this despite your years and many
lessons learned? Do you want your beard
laughing at you and brow's wrinkles
to be ashamed of you? Don't talk
so carelessly.

Joseph:
      I'll bear that in mind.
After all, it is vain of me
to believe such a thing of this child,
like it was the future Messiah.

Young Girl:
Why is such an enchanted glow
shining around the face of him?
From where beats this lovely shaft of light?
Or do my eyes play tricks on me?

Old Man:

>No, no, I see the glow now too.
>If the whole room's not bright with it,
>I'm blinded by an evil mirage.

Soldier:

>Yes, I see it too, and all can see,
>and all mankind to come will find
>this hour precious. Will he not draw
>everyone to him, who does not yet
>talk, but will one day speak of things
>divine? I am his prisoner
>and now regret all my past deeds.
>I marched through Galilee, Egypt,
>Syria. I left my regiment
>to greet this child. What a deep joy
>transfixes me before his image.
>I never trembled when in danger,
>me, the one who hurt so many.
>I have never shown emotion
>when they cried out that I spare them.
>Now what do I feel? Do I dream?
>Am I no longer the same man?
>Am I now another person,
>Someone higher?

Old Man:

>   No, one more gentle,
>and of course someone higher too.
>As you revere this young little creature,
>I, an old man, shall do so too.
>Have I, for as long as I've lived,
>seen a more beautiful moment?
>Have I ever known, as the whole world
>must by now, such a joyous event,
>such great hope? Someday it will be said

this was the time when love and faith
were born.

Joseph:

            Don't you go on and on,
almost like a boy or well-nigh
more. What is all this spirit for
tonight?

Mary:

            Likely they are all either
very mad or simply too overjoyed.
Could it be that God speaks from their mouths?

Joseph:

Would I know? I gave it no thought.
I've hardly seen anything odd
in these occurrences, not till
they said a miracle lives here.
That has got me shaking my head.
You know that I am, if anything,
a sensible man, someone who's
sober and thinks practically.
This childlike appearance, I myself
didn't take it all too much to heart.
"Well, it's a kid like any other.
Hopefully, he'll turn out just fine."
This is pretty much how I thought.
Now I'm nearly bewildered by their
dreamy talk, like I had indulged
in a heady drink. Still, I trust
in God.

Mary:

            Which is for the best too.
I'm pleased by how upright you are,
humble and good, as it should be.

One of the Kings:

>Let us kneel before the child
>and lay our gifts before him here
>at his feet.

>>*The Kings kneel.*

Joseph:

>>Worthy gentlemen,
>aren't you being a bit too polite?
>Don't you think you're being much too nice
>to me and my wife, to such plain
>and simple people as we are?

First King:

>It's for showing this devotion,
>and for this joyous arrival.
>If anything, it's just the way
>we decorate things. Such objects,
>as precious as they may seem to you,
>we have all over the place. So
>don't tell us how grateful you are.
>You've given us more, for we will
>bring this joy back to our homeland,
>for we have seen the Messiah,
>the Lord, in whom many people
>will one day have faith and build him
>a temple. However, he will
>not be so fortunate himself
>as one might think.

Mary:

>>What do you mean?

Second King:

>A smart man says nothing at all,
>not what he knows nor not what he
>thinks he might know.

First King:

                    You're right.
                    (To Mary) I meant
   only that your son, so great in love,
   could be like in suffering, nothing
   that might give you cause to worry.

Mary:

   Even as you give me joy, now you
   give me a heavy heart.

Third King:

                    It's nothing.
   He talks a bit too much.
                    (To his colleague) Better
   if you could keep it to yourself.

Mary:

   Suffering? Am I beginning
   to see what fate lies in store for my son?
   You look at me as though you cared
   for me, as though concerned, but what
   you're telling me doesn't sound pleasant.

Joseph:

   Peace and love and faith as well, go
   above all else.

Mary:

                    Of course, you good
   man.

Joseph:

        While it seems a trifle gloomy,
   things will soon be cheerful once more.
   We don't want to let our hearts get
   any sadder. After all, God has
   given this child to you, thus will

He lead it by the hand as well
through this unforeseeable life.

Old Man:
How serious everything is.

Jester:
Shall we be off?

Vagabond:
Someone surely
should make a start. Joy and sorrow,
greatness and baseness, are ever
cheek by jowl; this bit of wisdom
comes from a good-for-nothing's head.

Joseph:
Good night!

Soldier:
I'll be off too. Good night!

Third King:
We'll be wanting to go to our inn.

Old Man:
I should probably be going too.

Young Girl:
And I should do the same. Sleep well!

Joseph:
Well, they have all gone away now.

Mary:
Should we sleep too, like the others?
Surely you're a little tired from
talking to our guests. They gave you
so many things to think about.

Joseph:

Of course I'm a little sleepy,
but I'd rather you slept alone
and let me keep watch, so the child,
who they tell us is so special,
doesn't lack a faithful guardian.
Just close your eyes. Mine shall remain
open, so that nothing befalls
this gentleness, so that your dreams
are sweet and pleasant, with their shapes
calmly, lovingly wrapped around you.
Do not the stars watch outside too,
above our hill, this eternal soul
that is the spirit of the world,
that is this universe, this one
that never sleeps. Listen, who knocks
there at the door?

Angel:

You may lay
down, one mightier will keep watch.

Joseph:

I'll do what you tell me.

Angel:

Then you
do well.

Joseph:

Will this child be cared for?

Angel:

Be without worry, what you love,
and who's loved you, if you be true,
rest easy, thus you should too.

Joseph:
> Good night!

Mary:
> My faith is finally
> restored. Someday, when everything
> is not as nice as I would like
> to think, maybe this way I'll have
> the strength to bear it.

Joseph:
> So sleep well.

Angel:
> It's a very curious thing
> about the apprehensive minds
> of mortals, as though they always
> want to flee what's been decided
> on high, ever wanting to believe,
> putting everything in order,
> making extra work for themselves.
> Yet there are the good and the kind
> who do so, who don't want to sleep,
> for they think they will miss something.
> The Lord has dispatched me hither,
> so that I stand vigilant guard.
> It seems He holds both of them dear
> such that He'll go easy on them.
> Surely something special is in store
> for the little child, otherwise
> He'd not care so for the parents.
> Will He endow it with wisdom
> and beauty, prepare him for life's
> journey, which is aglow with great
> suffering, and then the heavy test,
> to claim for himself his divine,
> lofty, eternal dwelling place?